Promoting Effective Discipline in School and Classroom

A Practitioner's Perspective

Donald R. Grossnickle
Frank P. Sesko

Donald R. Grossnickle is assistant principal in charge of discipline at James B. Conant High School in Hoffman Estates, Ill., and adjunct assistant professor of curriculum at Northern Illinois University, DeKalb.

Frank P. Sesko is assistant principal in charge of discipline at Hoffman Estates (Ill.) High School.

Scott D. Thomson, *Executive Director*
Thomas F. Koerner, *Director of Publications*
Carol Bruce, *Assistant Director of Publications*
Patricia Lucas George, *Project Editor*

Copyright 1985
National Association of Secondary School Principals
1904 Association Drive, Reston, Virginia 22091

ISBN 0-88210-170-6

Contents

Acknowledgments

We would like to thank the following people for their assistance in making this publication possible: Jeannette Ciccia, Noble DeSalvi, Susan Johnstone, Joanne Mayer, Sally Ozga, and Mary Ann Sesko.

Foreword

No subject attracts as many readers among school practitioners as does *student discipline*. Although every school has its own administrative policies dealing with student disruption, educators continue to search for other ways—new techniques and different strategies—hoping to improve their own systems for handling discipline.

NASSP recognizes the need for schools to provide an orderly, safe, and stimulating educational environment for all youngsters and teachers. Research certainly supports the concept that the most effective learning occurs in such an environment. Consequently school people must be able first to analayze discipline problems accurately and then to counter them as quickly as possible.

Because we all realize that quick fixes do not exist, we accepted the proposal of Donald Grossnickle and Frank Sesko to prepare this monograph on this important subject. As assistant principals whose primary responsibility is discipline, they have written this material from a perspective only they and others in similar positions can have.

Promoting Effective Discipline in School and Classroom provides readers with a practical self-help guide. The authors provide readers with insights that will enable them to address the problems and promote effective discipline.

Thomas F. Koerner
Editor and Director
of Publications
NASSP

Chapter 1

Schoolwide and Classroom Discipline: A Teamwork Approach

Administering discipline is a more laborious task than taking refuge in a few simple punitive tricks. It is just as much more laborious and challenging as is modern medical thinking compared to the proud hocus-pocus of the primitive medicine man. The task of the teacher on his job is to translate the principles of democratic discipline into daily action in the classroom.[1]

One of the greatest challenges facing the school administrator each day is promoting a wholesome and supportive learning atmosphere throughout the school.

Promoting effective discipline in the school requires a comprehensive program supported by everyone in the entire school organization. Fundamental to achieving a school climate where teaching and learning occur with an absolute minimum of distraction is firm, consistent, and continuous commitment to the following:

- Mutual respect among students and staff
- Regard for the dignity of each person in the school

---

[1]Fritz Redl, *When We Deal with Children* (New York: Free Press, 1966), p. 254.

- Established standards and expectations to guide student conduct in classrooms and other areas of the school
- Commitment from every member of the school staff to support and enforce the discipline expectations and procedures established
- Effective instructional management and classroom control.

A well-disciplined school promotes the ideal of each student working toward self-management and controlling his or her own actions. At the same time, the school recognizes that adult intervention is both desirable and necessary.

As socializing institutions, schools accept the responsibility of helping each student to learn appropriate behavior as he or she develops into a mature member of society.

Reaching the goal of a well-disciplined school requires an honest, committed, and systematic effort to uncover new and better methods. We easily can be victims of our tendency toward habit and routine. Schools should select from a variety of new and emerging ideas and programs to revitalize the existing school discipline program.[2]

New emphasis on the role of the school counselor in discipline and ideas such as in-school suspension, contingency contracting, reality therapy, and other potential remedies provide options for improving the vitality of the existing discipline program when complete reform is not necessary. The three-step model described in this book provides the backbone of an effective approach to a comprehensive program for school discipline.

Many discipline problems can be minimized through prevention. Problem behavior should be handled quickly and decisively as administrators intervene and restore a supportive learning atmosphere.

Even the best ideas or programs cannot, in themselves, create this desired atmosphere in the school. Staff members must take charge of specific disciplinary procedures including the com-

[2]John F. Lordon describes a perspective that involves the "total school" in formulating discipline policy and procedures in *NASSP Bulletin*, April 1983, pp. 58-60.

prehensive disciplinary program. Individual commitment from every member of the staff is essential.

Disruptive behavior in schools historically has been a problem for school officials. We must not become overwhelmed by the public's outcry. Once we clearly understand the problems that exist, we can take the necessary steps to solve them.

Positive Classroom Management— The Teacher as the Key

The secret to establishing a successful classroom environment where little time is wasted because of disciplinary matters involves skillful teachers who can foster student involvement, cooperation, enthusiasm for learning, respect for fellow students and the teacher.

Effective classroom discipline management is closely related to the teacher's instructional effectiveness. Various researchers have identified characteristics of success and achievement-oriented classrooms. Essential elements include:

1. Effective means for establishing classroom procedures during the first weeks of school (See Appendix H)
2. A work-oriented but relaxed classroom climate
3. Clear and reasonable expectations, standards, and tasks
4. A predictable, consistent environment
5. Established consequences and rewards
6. Rationale for rules and procedures
7. Manageable activities organized to minimize confusion through clear directions and smooth transition from one activity to the next
8. Quick, quiet, calm behavior monitoring
9. Student input in selected classroom discussions
10. Accountability for assignment, tasks, and behavior
11. Feedback and praise
12. A variety of class activities
13. Attempts by the teacher to encourage and motivate students by taking a personal interest in each student
14. Teacher enthusiasm and love of the subject
15. Teacher goal to teach students the subject, not teach the subject to the student.

Teachers must be provided with exemplary resource teachers and knowledgeable administrators whom they can work with when attempting to resolve the inevitable discipline problems. In addition, both new teachers and veterans alike profit from well-planned and selected inservice materials and workshops in order to make effective strategies and techniques readily available.

Chapter 2
Simple Truths About School Discipline

A well-disciplined school:
- *Offers the same set of rules for everyone*
- *Provides equal application of all rules*
- *Depends on responsible students*
- *Guarantees a safe and comfortable environment*
- *Has a friendly and cooperative atmosphere*
- *Provides opportunities to lead and participate*
- *Allows time to accomplish goals*
- *Guarantees a real chance for success.*
Barrington (Ill.) High School Student Handbook

Teachers and administrators must search for assistance to help them improve classroom and school management skills. School discipline is sometimes overlooked in professional books, journals, teacher training courses, and teacher inservice activities because few people, it seems, want to focus attention on behavior problems.

Offering Practical Advice
Some "simple truths" concerning school discipline follow. The intent is to share state-of-the-art insights into discipline so educators can formulate alternative patterns for minimizing discipline problems in schools and classrooms.

40 Simple Truths About School Discipline

- *Most students are good in school and classroom situations.* The majority of students willingly and routinely adjust their own behavior without the need for external reminders or adult intervention. Anarchy, violence, and disruption are the exception rather than the rule.
- *Some students will exhibit problem behavior regardless of rules, procedures, and clear expectations.* A few students will make mistakes. Despite even their own good intentions, sometimes they are unwilling or unable to control their own behavior.
- *Most teachers can handle classroom discipline effectively through a variety of skills and techniques.* The majority of teachers are able to stimulate their students, motivate them, and create an atmosphere in which learning is the primary concern of students and the teacher.
- *Some teachers require extra assistance in developing discipline skills.* Due to a variety of reasons, including inadequate preparation in preventive discipline, some teachers may benefit from attending workshops and seminars, visiting other exemplary teachers' classrooms, and receiving help from school administrators.
- *Available materials and workshops on discipline are inadequate.* Both teachers and administrators report disappointment in the lack of useful publications and workshops organized to provide self-help guidance on discipline.
- *As teaching skills are developed, discipline problems decrease.* Teachers report that as they learn certain teaching techniques and use them effectively, they experience fewer discipline problems. Among skills frequently mentioned are: respect for students; bell-to-bell planning; interesting lessons that apply to student's lives and experiences; fewer teacher-dominated activities; realistic but challenging goals; fairness in grading practices; student involvement in planning class activities; and the use of common sense in minimizing problem behavior.
- *A minimum of rules should exist and those that do should be periodically reviewed.* Regular reviews should be con-

ducted in each school to assess the continued need for each rule.

- *All school and classroom rules must be effectively communicated.* It is everyone's responsibility to help students know what is acceptable behavior. Many modes of communication must be used. Emphasis should be made on avoiding punishment and teaching appropriate behavior.
- *Consequences for breaking school rules must be effectively communicated.* Most infractions should have specified consequences. This promotes consistent enforcement.
- *Existing rules must be firmly enforced.* The school must provide adequate personnel and resources to enforce school policies. This includes maintaining school records and efficient discipline office management. Teachers must know how they will be supported, and students must know that justice will be served swiftly and consistently.
- *Parents must be brought to school.* While the school may have been delegated to act in the place of the parent, the parent or guardian must assume primary responsibility to work with the school to assist in controlling their child's unacceptable behavior.
- *Some parents will disagree with school policy.* Some parents ask for strict discipline for their students, while others claim to be on the side of their child no matter what. Parents who may be emotional, irrational, and unaccepting of the school's policies should be treated courteously and with respect to the interests of their child as well as the interest of the school. Disagreement may be unavoidable, but cooperation is essential.
- *A relief valve can discourage "revolutionary" demands for change.* Keep in mind that students can "take over" a school if they want to. Provide readily available channels for voicing disagreements or complaints. The student protests of the past were said to be caused by insensitivity to student's rights as individuals. Create a relief valve.
- *Discipline enforcement must be consistent.* While there is always an appropriate time for compassion, specified penalties must be enforced whenever the infraction occurs. Some parents who formerly called for more dis-

cipline in schools demand leniency or request that the school overlook the matter when their child has committed an offense. Administrators must be firm with parents at times, too!

- *Conflict over interpretation of the seriousness exists.* The question of severity of the discipline infraction may vary among those involved in the situation. A detached but concerned perspective will minimize emotions and promote a just resolution of the problem for everyone.

- *The majority of school discipline problems are solved with the assistance of concerned and supportive parents.*

- *Some parents need to be reminded of the difficulty of operating a large school.* Some parents fault the school policies as being unnecessarily harsh when their students have committed offenses. These parents may benefit from a discussion of what it takes to provide a disciplined environment and how school rules may be different than those at home.

- *While it is the parents' right to disagree with a discipline decision, the student must know that the parent will cooperate with the school administrators.* If a student perceives an adversary relationship between parent and school, the student may take advantage of the situation, resulting in further misconduct. Visible disagreement should be minimized.

- *Some teachers assert that their only job should be to teach and wish to leave the discipline to the administration.* Teachers must be the first line of discipline. Good discipline starts with the effective teacher and should be the concern of all teachers.

- *Rules may create freedom.* If rules are made only to address problems and are kept to a minimum, good students who routinely exhibit responsible conduct in school may realize that they benefit from a quiet, disciplined atmosphere.

- *Students want limits.* Responsible students want to know what is expected so they can avoid "rubbing the teacher the wrong way." They appreciate knowing the limits.

- *School and classroom discipline is a local matter.* Parents and school officials should be aware of the wave of criticism of school discipline and judiciously respond only as the local situation requires.

- *Teachers must work together for consistency.* Students feel it unfair for one teacher to enforce a rule while another "looks the other way." Staff members suffer when some teachers play the role of "bad guys" who confront student behavior while others avoid getting involved.
- *Good discipline must be taught.* Don't assume that students know how to behave in various situations. Time and patience should be used as teachers and administrators help students learn why some behaviors are acceptable while others are not.
- *Preventive discipline means being positive.* Teachers should seek administrators' advice whenever possible to prevent the need for punishments. Encouragement instead of belittlement is the key.
- *Schools can help students learn social skills not learned at home.* Teachers should realize that because of the changes in the family and the effect on the home, the school may need to assist some students in developing social skills once taught by the family.
- *Schools require a supportive stance from parents, legislators, and courts.* Due process which protects the rights of students and parents should be given its "due," but should not promote an atmosphere of fear of reprisal for every disciplinary action taken.
- *Effective disciplinary practices are transferable.* A good idea, in the proper place, is a good idea. (Good ideas can come from other schools.)
- *Every group is different.* Every fall, a new group of students enters the classroom for the first time. Communicate to students that they are special by avoiding references to last year. Students can benefit from fresh starts and clean slates.
- *Teachers can make or break a new policy or program.* Foster teacher support for a new practice that can potentially solve a discipline problem. The program can fail if students perceive teachers do not support it. Teachers must be committed to the program.

- *Teachers expect to be supported by administrators.* When teachers perceive that the administrators don't care, their response is likely to be, "then why should I?" Such a problem is catastrophic to staff morale and must be confronted squarely and honestly.
- *Support staff should assist parents, teachers, and administrators.* When local funds allow, counselors, psychologists, and social workers should be employed to help solve discipline problems. Their help may provide solutions rather than just first aid measures such as punishment, suspension, and penalties.
- *Teachers want and have a right to be involved.* Involve teachers when considering discipline programs.
- *Good discipline in schools is firm, friendly, consistent, fair, and forceful.* After steps have been taken to deal with a disruptive student, it is sometimes necessary to be more forceful. While out-of-school alternatives such as suspension and expulsion are discouraged, a major change may be required for the overall good of the student and the school.
- *How teachers teach is just as important as the subject they teach.* Group work, student projects, encouragement, and support promote better student behavior.
- *Teachers and students should work toward common goals.* When students are involved in planning class activities, a spirit of cooperation exists which is far better than simple togetherness.
- *Teachers, administrators, and staff must model expected behavior.* Examine student scheduling, school size, curricula, school rules, and enforcement. The school must be a model to promote the best possible environment.
- *Schools should be places where parents can turn when their parenting skills do not seem to be working.* Although schools cannot solve all of a student's problems that surface in the home, the school may serve as a referral agency for outside counseling, parent support groups, and information concerning available research on child-rearing practices.
- *Periodic review of students exhibiting chronic behavior problems is important.* The counselor, disciplinarian, and teachers of the chronic "problem child" should meet to

evaluate progress, share ideas, and plan alternative approaches to help the student find success.

- *School and classroom programs should be initiated to encourage responsible behavior.* Students must have opportunities to make decisions about how to deal with any free time in their daily schedule. Programs such as study hall options or passes to leave class to work on other projects, emphasize the inherent good of students and support the concept that as students mature, they should become more responsible for their own actions.

Parents, teachers, students, and administrators all have a stake in the benefits derived from promoting well-disciplined schools. Local schools and communities must cooperate to define the role each will play in pledging consistent support for effective discipline policies, practices, and programs. Reform must be initiated by local boards of education, administrators, and teachers because no one is in a better position to improve discipline.

Chapter 3
Designing a Comprehensive Discipline Program

Ladies and Gentlemen of the Committee:

It is high time that we stop the nonsense in education and get down to basics. This is why we are gathered today as a discipline committee. After much discussion, thought, and contemplation, we feel, in our humble opinion, that we are conditioning and eventually graduating a large number of social misfits!

If a change in "tone," "conduct," "atmosphere," or "climate" is to take place in our students, it must be effected by the people who are going to execute the change: the teachers and staff! Who is better qualified than teachers and staff?

Our vested interest is the future of our community, our country, and our own school. If we want to establish ourselves and our school as a model, then we must work together—parents, community, and the Board of Education—to define and develop appropriate learning atmosphere within our school. We must consider the infractions of the rules, what should be done to remediate the problems and develop staff development proposals to guide the combined efforts of the staff....

William Severino and Ralph Losee
Teachers, J. B. Conant High School

Disruption and violence in the school cannot be tolerated if schools are to help young people learn.[1] Just as cancer must be isolated and treated in its early stages, so too must disruptive students be dealt with swiftly and firmly if schools are to remain healthy.

Schools are places where a few "good" kids sometimes act "bad," regardless of the prevalent disciplinary structures. At the heart of an effective discipline program are discipline strategies that transform inevitable student misbehavior into constructive, socially acceptable behavior.

A Systems Approach to Effective School Discipline

One such discipline program is a "systems" approach that is based on a three-part plan to establish effective discipline.

Part I: Identifying and subsequently eliminating the barriers to a positive learning atmosphere and instituting a preventive plan that avoids punishment.

Part II: Developing an intervention program that stops disruptive students from interfering with their own education or the education of others.

Part III: Using rehabilitation and therapy to resolve the student problems that cause disruption or violent behavior.

A Word of Caution: A word of caution is certainly in order to avoid over-reacting to the current focus on discipline.

Great strides have been taken to encourage a humanistic environment in schools characterized by positive student and teacher relationships based upon mutual respect and concern. Hostility, rebellion, defiance, and disrespect are present in some classrooms, and this must stop. The most important agenda is to help students achieve self-discipline and learn in a supportive, encouraging, and positive environment.

---

[1]See Robert J. Rubel, "Violence in Public Schools: HEW's Safe School Study," *NASSP Bulletin*, March 1978, pp. 75-83.

23 Essential Discipline Program Components

Schools must establish a "technology" of discipline procedures. These procedures, or components, use proven techniques to address discipline problems:

1. *School Discipline Philosophy*

   A school must develop a written discipline philosophy that serves as the foundation upon which all disciplinary actions should be based. The philosophy should be written with input from all members of the school staff. (See Appendix F for sample philosophy.)

2. *Administrative Guidelines for Discipline*

   Written policies and procedures that are to be administered by school officials should be available.[2] Essential guidelines include:
   - Responsibility of disciplinarian (job description)
   - Policy regarding behavior on the school bus and at special events/activities
   - Policy regarding the use of corporal punishment
   - Procedures for searches of students and lockers
   - Policy regarding attendance, truancy, tardiness, fighting
   - Student dress code
   - Statement concerning open and closed campus
   - Policy guiding the role of the police in the school
   - Procedures for providing due process in suspension and expulsion
   - Policy and procedures for dealing with the following common and recurring situations: academic problems, alcohol and drug abuse, theft, cheating, lying, forgery, dangerous behavior, insubordination, profanity/ obscenity, smoking, vandalism, and all offenses categorized as gross disobedience and misconduct.

3. *Student/Parent Handbook*

   The student handbook should be distributed to all students and their parents. The handbook should include all school rules and procedures, a description of the consequences for misbehavior, and the student code of conduct

[2]See William Fellmy, "Keys to Effective Discipline: Making Rules Simple, Clear, Visible," *NASSP Bulletin*, April 1983, pp. 68-70.

detailing how a student is expected to behave and describing the benefits of a well-disciplined school.

4. *Clear Expectations for Student Behavior*
A specific plan to communicate behavior expectations should be developed, implemented, and periodically revised. The following is a sample communication plan:

Students

- District sends a handbook home
- A slide/tape presentation about student rights and responsibilities is viewed by students in study halls during the first weeks of school
- Slide/tape presentation on class, hallway, bus, cafeteria behavior may also be used
- Administrators visit study halls first week of *each* semester to explain rules
- Teachers "teach" expected behavior during first week of *each* semester.

Administrators

- Administrators communicate to staff members the expected student behavior and method of teaching this behavior
- Faculty/staff members receive guidelines about what steps to take to enforce appropriate behavior and what kind of follow-up can be expected from administrators
- Administrators orient supervisors and bus drivers regarding expected behavior.

Parents

- Summer newsletter discusses expected behavior
- Parent receives student/parent handbook at the beginning of the school year
- Special mailings are continued throughout school year
- Assistant principal talks to parents at open house.

5. *Teacher Handbook with Specific Guidelines and Procedures for Dealing with Discipline*
Specific guidelines provided to the teacher may include:
- Teacher responsibility in classroom discipline (description of the teacher's role and the administrator's role)

- Guidelines for preventive discipline
- Guidelines for handling serious discipline problems and violence
- Guidelines for how and when to refer a student to the office
- A list of the steps prescribed for each of the most common and recurring discipline infractions and a list of responses teachers can expect for each offense
- Procedures for handling students suspected of drug and alcohol use
- Guidelines for how to get help in an emergency

6. *Effective Attendance Procedures*
   The school should know the whereabouts of every student in the school at all times. In the case of absence, parents are to be quickly notified if the parent has not called the school. Teachers must take accurate attendance and send students to the office to be accountable for unexplained absences.

7. *A Variety of Available Interventions*
   Detention is a somewhat effective penalty for infractions that are related to tardiness or truancy. Penalties for other misbehaviors include after-school conference with the teacher, reduction of free time after lunch, etc.

8. *Systematic Recordkeeping*
   Well-designed forms can be the difference between effective and ineffective discipline programs. Effective use of the proper forms helps each member of the staff know what is going on in order to assist a student with a problem. When a disciplinary action is taken, the student is accountable to all those who receive a copy of the referral.

9. *Support Services*
   When good students misbehave, it is often because the student has a conflict that requires the services of the psychologist, social worker, school nurse, counselor, special educator, police consultant, or disciplinarian. These support services are important.

10. *Closed Campus*
    Once students come to school, they should stay there until the conclusion of their classes. Closed campus reduces the possibility that students might "find trouble,"

return to school late, not return to school, or return under the influence of drugs or alcohol.

11. *Outreach Programs*

The school should recognize the need for special services that can be provided outside the typical services of the counseling staff. Since students' lives are frequently troubled by personal problems, students should be directed toward some of these outside services such as peer counseling, family counseling, Alcoholics Anonymous, Narcotics Anonymous, and other types of local support groups. Some communities have programs for potential dropouts and those who require special motivation.

12. *Alternative Education Opportunities*

An alternative learning school provides short-term instruction for students who might otherwise be academically unsuccessful. The goal is to return students to their home school with earned credits, improved self-esteem, improved attendance, increased willingness to accept authority, and a better opportunity to learn and succeed.

13. *Periodic Review of Discipline and Attendance Statistics*

Administrators should periodically summarize types of discipline referrals and attendance statistics in order to evaluate the direction in which the school is proceeding. It would be beneficial to keep such statistics from year to year and to make periodic comparisons to enable administrators to see whether the overall climate of the school is constant or changing and whether they should restructure discipline or attendance procedures. These periodic reviews should be shared with teachers. (See Appendix E)

14. *Inservice/Staff Development*

An ongoing program of staff inservice is a vital part of an effective and productive learning institution. The program must consist of three basic elements:

A. Orientation of new teachers to include the following:
- The goals and aspirations of the school
- School policies and regulations
- The names of fellow teachers, support service personnel, cafeteria and maintenance personnel
- Location and use of classroom, cafeteria, library, teachers' lounge, and lavatories

- Courses of study, guidebooks, textbooks, and supplementary materials for grade or subject
- Attendance reports, pupil and school records, requisition forms, plan books, etc.
- Methods of ordering books and supplies, securing audiovisual equipment, duplicating material, disposing of lost and found articles
- Schedule and meaning of all audio signals
- Regulations for pupils in building and on school grounds; uses of entrances, exits, lavatories, outdoor areas, equipment and activities; regulations for pupils during, before, and after school hours
- Procedures and policies regarding teacher meetings, inservice training, absence, attendance, and dismissal
- Emergency procedures including fire drills, severe weather alerts, bomb scares.

B. Opportunities for staff training, preparation, instruction, and communication to include the following:

- Opportunities for teachers to have access to classrooms and department offices when the school is closed during the summer, on weekends, and during winter and spring breaks
- Work days at the beginning of the school year to give direction, set goals, refresh procedures, and review plans for preventive discipline
- Monthly faculty meetings before or after school for the entire faculty or on a revolving meeting schedule throughout the day for small groups to express concerns, discuss possible solutions, praise progress, highlight programs, give inservice training, review discipline statistics, and share insights
- Monthly department meetings to share ideas, express concerns, discuss solutions, promote consistency, and highlight innovative ideas
- Monthly meetings for supervisory, clerical, and custodial staffs to become aware of upcoming activities, express concerns, discuss possible solutions, and have inservice training
- Two or three yearly opportunities for the entire staff to meet socially

- Opportunities for teachers and counselors to observe disciplinarians at work in a shadow program.
  C. An end-of-the-year, all-staff members meeting to include each of the following:
    - A review of the year's outstanding accomplishments
    - Recognition of outstanding teacher and support staff service including attendance, awards, recognitions, longevity of service, and retirements
    - Words of encouragement and appreciation from the principal.

15. *Effective Means for Parent Involvement*
Parents must be kept informed of total school/district activities through use of:
    - Student/parent calendar handbook
    - Quarterly newsletters from the superintendent
    - Monthly newsletters from the principal
    - At least one annual open house
    - Parental contact before minor classroom problems become major
    - Mid-quarter progress reports or special commendations
    - Confidential discipline notices
    - Promotion of booster club, PTA or PTO, etc.
    - Awards nights to recognize students for outstanding accomplishments.

16. *Student Identification Card*
All students should be furnished with a picture I.D. which they must carry at all times. In addition to their name, address, and picture, the card should list first class starting time, lunch period, and last class ending time. The card may also be used to show special privileges such as off-campus lunch permission, smoking area privileges, library privileges, etc. The more the card is utilized by the school, the more students will remember to carry it at all times. Such a system also makes it easier to identify unauthorized visitors.

17. *Effective Supervision of School Property*
Effective building supervision by teachers or other adults hired as paraprofessional supervisors will help to keep students under control, keep unwelcome outsiders away,

reduce vandalism, and add to the educational atmosphere of the school. Specific areas for supervision are halls, cafeteria, washrooms, entrances and exits, and parking lots.

18. *Custodial and Maintenance Program*
A custodial staff should be dedicated to a program of preventive maintenance. Lights must be replaced as soon as they are burned out or broken. Graffiti must be cleaned off immediately.

19. *Supportive Principal and Staff*
If the principal instructs the staff about preventive discipline techniques and expects the staff to follow those techniques, the principal must support teachers and supervisors in their efforts to maintain control and improve instruction. If a classroom teacher, for instance, has made every effort to minimize discipline problems in the classroom, has held student conferences, has contacted parents, has sought assistance from the counselor, and has finally had to refer a student to a principal, assistant principal, or dean, that teacher *must* be supported in his or her actions.

20. *Supportive Board of Education and Adequate Legal Counsel*
In the same way that teaching and support staff members must be able to count on the principal for support, so too must the principal be able to count on backing from district administrators and the board of education. The board of education must have a well-defined discipline policy that allows enough latitude for administrative discretion. That policy must enable rather than thwart fair, firm, friendly, and consistent discipline. When administrators who have worked within the confines of those policies come up against resistant parents, the board of education must consistently support those administrative decisions. The board must also be prepared to back that support with adequate legal counsel.

21. *Supportive and Capable Disciplinarians with Strong Public Relations Skills*
When considering employing a disciplinarian, the super-

intendent and the principal should strongly consider promoting someone from within the district. No one should be better equipped to understand the problems of a particular school district than someone from that district. Consideration should be given not only to persons with capable management skills, but also persons who have been successful teachers. Backgrounds in counseling and parenting also prove helpful, and strong, positive communication skills are essential.

22. *A Procedure for Students To Voice Opinions*
Students have the right to be treated justly. If a student feels that he or she has been treated unjustly, the case may be appealed to the following people in the order listed:
- Teacher or staff member whose action is being questioned
- Assistant principal
- Superintendent or assistant
- Board of education through its hearing officer, whose sole duty is to report such incidents to the board.

At each level of appeal, a decision will be made. Should that decision be unacceptable to the student, he or she may appeal to the next level of authority. The decision of the board of education must be considered the final action of the district.

Students are responsible for being aware of and following district policies and procedures in all matters that pertain to them. Students are expected to use good judgment before making charges of unjust treatment.

When confronted by a staff member about misbehavior or misconduct, students should be advised not to argue or escalate the matter. If they disagree with the staff member, they should do so courteously or report to the office. They should never leave a class to solve a dispute. Students should be advised to always try to resolve the problem with the person involved before appealing.

23. *An Athletic and Activities Program*
Student activities are an integral part of our educational

plan. Not only should schools produce citizens able to perform the tasks essential to the present and future demands of our society, but they should help develop social skills.

Chapter 4
Establishing a Positive Approach

"School conflicts cannot be expected to vanish of their own accord but should be brought out in the open and managed by providing channels or occasions through which adversaries can introduce their conflicting claims into the business of the school."

Schmuck et al., *The Second Handbook of Organizational Development in Schools*, 1977, p. 191

Parents, teachers, and even students seem to agree about the most desirable climate or atmosphere for learning. In general terms:

- Students should learn in a democratic environment
- Schools should establish a supportive climate
- Schools should focus on positive behavior and help to build students' self-confidence and self-worth
- Students should learn in an orderly non-threatening environment
- Schools should allow students to live in a self-disciplined climate.

An effective school discipline program is perhaps best based on these general guiding principles, but teachers and administrators must translate these general goals into specific steps for implementing a total school discipline program.

Schools as organizations must deal with daily conflict about individual student needs versus the needs of the staff members and other students. This situation is not only inevitable, but normal and natural. Recognizing the apparent potential for conflict, school administrators and teachers should identify specific practices that prevent and resolve problems with the least amount of time and energy.

Creating a Learning Atmosphere

The effective school discipline program is based on an on-going effort to:

1. Prevent discipline problems before they happen
2. Intervene so that conflict among organizational needs and student needs are eliminated using problem-solving techniques
3. Eventually resolve a "discipline problem" by focusing on the causes and providing therapeutic assistance to search for a satisfactory resolution.

The model for designing an effective discipline program is provided in Figure 1, which specifies the components and how each fits into an overall program to promote a disciplined school.

The three key elements of the model: prevention, intervention, and resolution, are not all that is required to achieve a school that promotes discipline and learning. This systematic

Figure 1

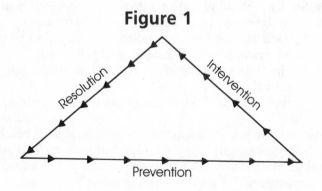

approach also requires that the discipline program be organized based on specific standards for learning and behavior.

In order for teachers to be effective and for students to learn, a good discipline program will utilize the following:

- Agreed-upon discipline philosophy
- Communication of the standards of proper conduct
- Supportive staff
- Enforced consequences for misbehavior
- Commitment to helping solve problems of students with special needs
- A variety of skills useful in managing class behavior
- A vital curriculum
- Respectful and dignified treatment of students.[1]

Long-term reform built on a foundation of accepted philosophy and adopted policy, standards, and procedures is the best way to promote the climate that encourages successful learning in a supportive environment.

Climbing the Discipline Program Ladder

School administrators often envision a school environment free of discipline problems, but they are unsure about the steps that must be taken to achieve their goal. Figure 2 illustrates a step-by-step conceptualization of the process that moves a school toward a more disciplined climate.

---

[1]A model program that promotes understanding of students and self-concept developmental activities is described in the September 1979 *NASSP Bulletin*, pp. 27-33, by Diane Frey and Joseph Young.

Figure 2

Developing a Complete School Discipline Program:
A Step-by-Step Approach

Step

10 . . . . Learning successfully . . . .

9 . . . . Teaching effectively . . . .

8 . . . . Creating the tone of . . . .
positive learning environment

7 . . . . Resolving problems . . . .

6 . . Establishing resources to help resolve the causes of
misbehavior and assist students with their special needs
and problem . . . .

5 . . . . . . Establishing an intervention and enforcement
approach using conflict management and problem-
solving techniques . . . .

4 . . . . Implementing a preventive discipline program . . . . .

3 . . . . . . Identifying school and classroom discipline . . . .

2 . . . . Adopting a discipline philosophy . . . .
based on community values . . . .

1 . . . . Adopting a philosophy and . . . .
instructional goals for
the entire school
curriculum

Chapter 5
Designing a Preventive Discipline Program

Inevitably, now and then a group of "good kids" will misbehave. Therefore, it seems logical to prevent or at least minimize behavior problems before punishment is necessary.

Preventive medicine and preventive safety and maintenance programs are all based on the idea that the best "cure" is to avoid potential problems.
This management practice saves effort, time, inconvenience, and most important, increases organizational effectiveness.

Students are bound to make mistakes as they learn to choose between right and wrong. The school's responsibility is to provide necessary support, guidelines, and encouragement as students become self-disciplined and behave with regard to both personal goals and concern for others.

The following list identifies responsibilities of teachers and administrators that may promote effective discipline in school and classroom.

Major Responsibilities of Teacher
- Instructing using a variety of approaches that can be linked to the students' life experiences
- Anticipating opportunities for misbehavior and planning to avoid it
- Communicating what is expected of students

- Establishing fair, clearly understood grading practices
- Promoting student input and involvement and de-emphasizing teacher-dominated activities
- Encouraging daily attendance
- Making students aware of the teacher's pet peeves without their having to discover them in error
- Providing praise, recognition, and reinforcement.

Major Responsibilities of Administrator

- An established discipline philosophy to guide action
- Written discipline policies, procedures, and consequences for misbehavior
- Curriculum that assists in proper placement of students according to ability
- Effective counseling program for students and parents promoting selection of courses that interest students
- Opportunities for students to work on problems that interfere with their effectiveness as students, such as groups for students experiencing the pain of divorce in the family and/or family alcoholism
- Open lines of communication between teachers and parents
- Adequate policy involvement to ensure a secure and safe environment
- A process to review cases involving students who exhibit chronic problem behavior in order to share information and insights and recommend alternative strategies
- Procedures to deal effectively with drug and alcohol problems.

Shared Responsibilities of Teacher and Administrator

- Communication of expectations
- Effective relationships between students and teachers
- A business-like atmosphere

- Enforcement of all existing rules
- Parental involvement
- Minimal rules and emphasis on communicating the reasons for adopted rules
- Opportunities for legitimate involvement of students in decisions that affect them
- No favoritism or special treatment
- No ridicule, scolding, or public humiliation
- An atmosphere of helping the students achieve their goals
- No threats that will not or cannot be enforced
- No punishing the entire group for infractions of a few
- No dwelling on past mistakes
- No trying to be viewed as a "buddy"
- Humor
- No sarcasm
- Little emphasis on the use of power and authority in order to control
- Opportunities for students to demonstrate self-discipline and exhibit responsibility
- Emphasis on a positive viewpoint, building self-esteem
- Opportunities for students who have misbehaved to reestablish the respect and confidence of the teacher once it is temporarily lost due to an incident
- Planning for special days, fire drills, day before vacation
- Planning for substitute teachers
- Minimum force to quell discipline problems
- Motivational activities
- Opportunities to recognize students for doing good deeds and praise them by reinforcing their good behavior
- Common sense before allowing a situation to escalate to the point where damage is due
- Reminders to students about the way that their behavior is perceived by others
- Punishment and penalties that fit the misbehavior
- Significant penalties that deter misbehavior while avoiding "overkill"
- Freedom to acknowledge and admit mistakes
- Private scoldings, conferences.

Classroom Management

The key to effective school discipline is the effective management of classroom discipline before the problem is sent to the school office. The classroom management procedure is built on a philosophy of applying a minimum amount of force and gradually increasing levels of authority as misbehavior persists.

At the same time, administrators should make conscious efforts to identify common "pitfalls" or obstacles to student discipline. While experience may be the best teacher in many cases, an approach that avoids conflict ensures more time for learning and less time for trouble.[1]

Utilizing a Preventive Approach

A preventive approach to discipline communicates to students that the focus of school discipline is to promote success, not to punish. The plan is simple:

Minor classroom misbehavior should be handled by a direct verbal warning. If a teacher has developed the proper rapport in the classroom and has the respect of the students, the situation should be easily corrected.

If the student continues to create a class disturbance or fails to cooperate, the student remains after class for a conference. The teacher should inform the student why the behavior is intolerable and evaluate the outcome of the conference. The student must understand that she or he sacrifices the valuable learning time of each member of the class. The Classroom Management Form (see Appendix A) should be used to record the specifics of the conference.

A second conference with a student should be scheduled if the student does not respond or improve, tends toward academic deterioration, and/or has a generally disrespectful, disruptive, or insubordinate attitude. One day's notice must be

---

[1]B. J. Marcus, "Discipline and the School Calendar," *NASSP Bulletin*, February 1977, pp. 88-90; L. Clark, "Trends in Student Behavior," *NASSP Bulletin*, February 1984, pp. 27-28.

given before a conference is scheduled, and the department's office is the recommended site for the conference. Level Two of the Classroom Management Form should be completed. A written agreement (including consequences) may be required from the student. (See Appendix B)

Teachers are encouraged to use the guidance personnel as basic resources in seeking to understand the particular problems of a student.

The department chairperson may be consulted for advice and help in handling any type of discipline problem. The department chairperson may not be a direct-line disciplinarian, but his or her experience may help the teacher resolve classroom behavioral problems. On occasion, however, the chairperson may want to participate in an after-school conference with both the teacher and the student.

The steps outlined should be adequate to handle most classroom situations. It is hoped that the student's misbehavior will be corrected before referral to an assistant principal/dean. For the "hardcore" discipline cases, completion of the Classroom Management Form provides for background data which may be needed to take appropriate actions such as removing disruptive students from class.

Preventive discipline also ensures that the teacher has the skill to differentiate between those incidents that should be handled in the classroom and those that are best referred to others. Teachers should be provided with written guidelines such as the following:

A student may be sent to the office any time that student's conduct becomes so disruptive or offensive that it is impossible to conduct a class in an orderly fashion. In this situation, complete a referral form and send that student to the office.

EXAMPLE: The teacher has told the student to "stop chatting," and, getting no response, asks the student to move to a different seat. The student refuses. The teacher should immediately fill out a referral form and send the form and the student to the office or notify the office to send an administrator to the classroom.

The following incidents should result in immediate referral:
1. Smoking in school

2. Fighting (anywhere on school ground or the bus)
3. Directing profanity at a teacher or supervisor
4. Vandalizing
5. Threatening or actual violence directed toward a teacher
6. Possessing or being under the influence of controlled substance
7. Cheating
8. Insubordination
9. Stealing.

To clarify the teacher's role in handling discipline, guidelines should be provided and explained in the teachers' handbook. The following case study illustrates a sample process that seeks to identify and solve a problem using the minimum level of force. This systematic process may guide the teacher in helping to interrupt a troublesome student before involving parents or administrator.

Case Study 1

Joe is a junior in Miss Devine's sophomore remedial reading class. This is his second attempt at passing the class. He knows well the good behavior that Miss Devine expects of her students.

On the first day of class, as Miss Devine is going over the course outline and the sheet which explains her classroom rules and regulations, Joe already begins to exhibit some unacceptable behavior. Joe is leaning back in his chair, putting his feet up on the desk, and is tearing off bits of paper which he rolls into little balls and flips onto the desk of the timid girl who sits next to him.

As Miss Devine is going over the prepared sheets with the class, she moves about the room, eventually placing herself next to Joe, who momentarily stops tossing the bits of paper. Without a word, she motions Joe to put his feet on the floor. She points to the rule which the class has been going over as she continues the review. She remains at Joe's side for a few moments. If possible, she tries to involve Joe in the discussion of the rules, careful to avoid asking him to read anything aloud that he might not be able to handle and which would embarrass him.

When class is dismissed, she asks Joe to remain after for a moment. If he protests that he will be late for his next class, she offers to write him a pass to excuse his lateness.

Then, with no other students around, she says to Joe, "Joe, I'd really like to help you to pass this course, but I'm going to need your cooperation."

After getting by the initial, "What'd I do?" discussion, Joe finally says, "I just get bored. I didn't even think about what I was doing."

"I'll tell you what I'm going to do for you," says Miss Devine. "We'll try to work on a code system. If you start doing something you shouldn't, I'll just come by your desk and touch you on the shoulder. That should be enough to let you know that I don't like what you're doing and that I want you to stop it. So long as you stop, the incident will be over. If I have to stop you twice in a period, I'll have to see you after class. If it were to continue, I'd have to call your parents. Joe, you are a young adult. That's how I'd like to treat you. I can do that if you let me. Only if you don't accept that responsibility do I have to contact your parents."

To further assist Joe, Miss Devine may then tell Joe that she plans to call on him the next day to read a given paragraph. If Joe can look over the paragraph the night before, he may feel more relaxed the next day when called on to read. That may increase his confidence level in himself and may improve his attitude toward the class.

Case Study 2

A high school English teacher had the following plan for dealing with disruptive students.

Step 1: Minor class disruptions would be met with an in-class warning. (Note: While occasional minor disturbances may be overlooked, major disruptions may call for an immediate referral to an administrator.)

Step 2: A student guilty of repeated disturbances who did not heed in-class warnings would be asked to remain after class.

Step 3: After class the teacher would identify the problem. The student may be asked to supply a solution, or the teacher might suggest a specific nonverbal warning system to use for that particular student, i.e., a tap on the desk, touch on the shoulder.

Step 4: Failure to respond to the nonverbal warning would call for an after school conference and parent contact.

Step 5: The administrator would be advised of the misconduct and the steps taken to correct the behavior.

Step 6: Any further disturbances would call for an immediate referral to the administrator.

Note: Actions that interfere with other students' learning or that prevent the teacher from teaching must not be tolerated.

Chapter 6
Establishing a Preventive Approach: Schoolwide Model

Administrators' handling of such minor problems as students who are unprepared for class or students who do not have completed homework assignments not only takes an excessive amount of administrators' time, but makes frequent visits to the disciplinarian's office a common occurrence and no great cause for concern in the minds of the students.

Furthermore, it renders teachers ineffective by stripping them of even more power within the classroom.

To address this problem, the principal and the administrators who deal with discipline should work with teachers to design a complete program of preventive discipline.

The primary purposes of such a program are to make classroom teachers feel more in control of their classrooms, and to free administrators to handle more serious discipline problems and to focus on attendance issues. Thus, teachers and administrators work cooperatively with parents to produce responsible, self-disciplined young adults.

The first step of the plan is to discuss major discipline concerns at general faculty meetings. Time must then be spent with the staff members discussing their ideas about what constitutes good discipline. The third step is to discuss the types of misbehaviors that the staff members feel call for immediate disciplinary action. The fourth and final step requires the staff members to agree about who should have the disciplinary role.

Standards for Success

For example, one school staff established three basic categories of discipline concerns. The first deals with very minor discipline infractions that would call for teacher discretion as to whether the incident called for a reprimand or a warning by the teacher, or perhaps should be overlooked. Such infractions may include talking in class or study hall, failing to bring supplies to class, throwing papers in class, running in the halls, etc.

The second category deals with types of discipline for which some response must be made. The type of response would depend on the degree of severity of the discipline infraction. These types of behavior might include insubordination, horseplay, rudeness, pushing and shoving, profanity, etc.

The third category calls for an automatic referral to a disciplinarian. Such infractions include fighting, smoking, vandalism, and substance use. Whatever the level of discipline concern, the handling of that concern must be fair, firm, friendly, and consistent.

The entire staff may then agree to implement some basic standards for success to be implemented in the forthcoming school year. The staff, for example, may agree on four minimal standards for each and every classroom. Students should be informed of these standards and they should be posted in each classroom. These standards might be:

1. To be present and on time
2. To bring learning materials
3. To exhibit respect for other people and their property
4. To be prepared to participate.

Based on those four basic standards for success, each department should be required to develop its own departmental classroom standards. The objective is to have each department more clearly define each of these basic standards as they relate to their department.

For instance, in classes such as English, social science, and math, teachers may define a tardy policy as, "Students must be in their seats when the tardy bell begins to sound." Art teachers, on the other hand, might state, "Students must be at their work stations getting materials ready when the tardy bell begins to sound." The physical education department might say, "Students must be in the locker room when the tardy bell begins to sound." (See Appendix G)

While because of different classroom situations there could not be the same consistency from department to department, there must be consistency within departments. Teachers should be encouraged to expand further on classroom standards within their individual classrooms.

Teachers should also be encouraged to discuss individual discipline concerns with administrators or department chairpersons, and should be encouraged to contact parents before problems get out of hand.

Minor discipline problems should not be dealt with by administrators unless teachers first meet with the student outside of class and call the parent in an attempt to resolve the problem. Teachers are also strongly encouraged to involve the student's counselor in recurrent minor behavior problems.

In order for such a prevention program to be successful, 10 basic elements are essential:

1. Careful planning of a preventive discipline program
2. An effective supervisory plan for halls, cafeteria, and all areas of the facility
3. An orientation to the program for all staff members including supervisory personnel
4. An orientation program for students to include a well-planned, easily read student/parent handbook and individual classroom standards
5. Well-informed parents
6. A teaching staff dedicated not only to improvement of behavior, but to improvement of instruction as well
7. Building administrators who stand behind the teaching staff and who offer support whenever needed
8. Central office administrators who give their endorsement to the program and who are willing to continue endorsing the program even under fire from the disgruntled few
9. A board of education that is willing to back its admin-

istrators and to trust their professional judgments
10. Periodic reinforcement and review of the program through inservice and proper orientation of new staff members.

Without each of these elements, it would be difficult if not impossible for a program of preventive discipline to work successfully. It is also most important that the teaching staff, administrators, and board of education members realize that because the program has been successful for a time, it still requires periodic re-evaluation.

Note: This model for establishing a schoolwide approach to preventive discipline was based upon a successful program utilized at Hoffman Estates (Ill.) High School.

Chapter 7

Discipline Intervention: Putting a Stop to Discipline Problems

SPECIAL QUALITIES OF A DEAN

A dean must have an understanding of youth. He must have a sincere love for young people, a willingness to accept them as they are, and a desire to help them with their problems. In dealing with youth, teaching experience and a pleasant disposition are two essential qualities a dean should possess. He must be cognizant of the oppression of adolescents. He must be able to punish students without antagonizing them. He must be fair to all students. The dean must relate well with teenagers in many different settings. The ability to make quick sound judgments is necessary. He must have a wide range of knowledge with which to deal with thirteen-year-olds as well as adults. He must be able to inspire parents to work with the school for the good of their children. The dean needs to understand the social, economic, religious background of the community, have a sincere belief in the value of public school education, and have faith in the triumph of good over evil. The dean must possess good common sense and be able to get along with the faculty with a minimum amount of stress. He must set the example and be able to take criticism, even though it may be unjust. He must be diplomatic, as well as strict, sympathetic, and tactful. He must view problems objectively and see the total school when making a decision. He must maintain low blood pressure, a low boiling point, and an ability to leave problems at school. A dean must possess understanding of human frailties. He must be confident in his abilities and know his weaknesses. And most of all, he cannot take himself too seriously. (G. D. Vena, Arlington (Ill.) High School)

Administrator's Role in Discipline

The school office is generally considered the place where misbehavior is handled. To many, it represents an ominous, mysterious place where students are sent for a cure. The fact is, most students and teachers never actually experience a "session in the office."

When several students and staff members were asked, "What happens to students who are sent to the office?" the following responses were given:

- Teacher: "They're disciplined and helped."
- Student: "They yell at you."
- Teacher: "They get what is coming to them."
- Student: "We get punished."
- Teacher: "Rules are enforced and penalties given."
- Student: "I don't know, but it is usually bad."
- Teacher: "They have done something wrong; they should get justice tempered with mercy."

From an administrators' viewpoint, the discipline office is more than a place where penalties are doled out. It is more like a hospital emergency room instead of a simple treatment room where students get their "due."

The school administrator who is responsible for handling the discipline in the school functions as a catalyst who is supposed to get things done, thereby freeing the classroom and school from disruptions, crime, and violence.

The role of the disciplinarian requires enough flexibility to both follow board policy and administrative guidelines, and exercise administrative discretion. Essentially, the disciplinarian is supposed to enforce the rules; however, rarely is he or she provided with specific procedures to accomplish the task.[1]

Consider the diverse characteristics of a disciplinarian. Certainly, the job description calls for a man/woman for all seasons: prosecutor, judge, jury, defense attorney, counselor, peacemaker, teacher of teachers, problem solver, detective, humanitarian, and first and foremost, a champion of order and control for school and classroom.

When "bad" students are sent to the office, a preliminary screening or assessment is the first step to identifying the problem. Some students can be taken care of with minimal "first aid" measures. Others require radical treatment such as expulsion, suspension, and even arrest. Some students require the attention of specialists.

In any case, the assistant principal, dean, vice principal, or principal is expected to solve the problem so that the teacher can teach without disruption and students can concentrate on learning.

Administrative Discipline Tools

The disciplinarian has available a number of intervention tools, or "tricks of the trade." The following is a brief list of some common discipline techniques used in intervention procedures:

- Detention
- Suspension (out-of-school and in-school)
- Expulsion
- Conference with teacher, student, parent, and/or administrator
- Removal of student from class without credit
- Denial of privileges
- Contingency contract
- Reprimand and warning
- Motivational pep talk

---

[1]J. Patrick Mahon in the February 1979 *NASSP Bulletin* (pp. 68-73), describes a good summary of the relationship of student discipline intervention and legal guidelines.

In-School Suspension

An in-school suspension program (described in Appendix D) is an effective method for dealing with disruptive students. Before a student is assigned to in-school suspension, a parent conference sets the stage for building a cooperative relationship between students, parents, and the school. The time away from classes demonstrates to the students that if they wish to be members of the school community, they must earn their way back in. The point is made: Either conform to the rules or be taken out of the school, possibly permanently.

A counseling period provides the opportunity to help the student learn why he or she misbehaves, what is expected, and how future problems can be avoided. Most important, students do not like the isolation of in-school suspension and will consider it an unpleasant consequence of disruptive or violent behavior.[2]

Contingency Contract

One successful means of identifying and clarifying inappropriate behavior to a student and his or her parents is the behavioral contingency contract, which clearly specifies the consequences of misbehavior. A student agrees that if he or she continually misbehaves in a class, he or she can be removed from that class. Students appreciate being able to help develop a new plan to avoid further conflict, and parents appreciate being involved in the situation before their student is removed from the class. A sample generalized form is included. (See Appendix C.) Other statements may also be added to customize the contract.

Out-of-School Suspension/Explusion— Last Resort

Vandals, drug distributors, arsonists, and chronic fighters have no place in the traditional public school, and may require

---

[2]John A. Pare describes yet another discipline tool for administrators in the design of alternative learning centers in the April 1983 *NASSP Bulletin*, pp. 61-67.

outside help during suspension or expulsion. Suspension and expulsion serve as a last resort to protect students, staff, and school property, and ensure an orderly and effective learning environment.

Suspension and expulsion are extreme means of dealing with serious problems that threaten the effectiveness of the school program. Although they do have disadvantages, these measures can and should be used judiciously. Some of the advantages of suspension are:

1. Other students and teachers do not have to suffer because someone is not interested in learning.
2. The student and parents recognize that misbehavior cannot/will not be accepted in the school and classroom.
3. Suspension provides an opportunity to invoke the cooperation of parents, the student, and school staff in improving the offender's destructive behavior patterns.
4. Suspension is instructive to other students and functions as a deterrent for those tempted to misbehave.

Fortunately, the disciplinarian does not normally function alone. Administrators may call on the school psychologist, counselors, social workers, or juvenile police officers when students' problems must be resolved. In intervention procedures, the primary goal is to restore order and control into the classroom and school setting as quickly and painlessly as possible by resolving students' problems.

Teacher Input: Key to Successful Intervention

Anyone who has been a disciplinarian will admit that the most difficult and challenging task of that job is to solve problems while satisfying those being served. To please some of the people some of the time is just not good enough for the conscientious administrator.

Students who are punished are often unhappy with solutions developed by the disciplinarian, and parents, while stating that there should be more discipline in the schools, often disagree openly with the punishment imposed on their misbehaving children.

What is perhaps most distressing to the school administrators who are in charge of discipline is that often teachers express dissatisfaction or disagreement with the final disciplinary action taken, saying that they feel unsupported or double-crossed.

Administrators must often rely on incomplete information when dealing with disruptive students. In the rush to send a problem student to the office, teachers may not relay all of the details of the incident so necessary to making a fair decision about disciplinary action.

Administrators must resist the temptation to make decisions based on only the facts on hand and must instead insist on obtaining the complete story before deciding about punishments.

Complete, well-detailed referrals may make it possible for the administrator to deal with the incident immediately, and expediency makes discipline far more meaningful.

Time, or lack of it, strongly affects the way school administrators make decisions about discipline. Regardless of the extra time that may be required to gather complete information and the effort required by the referring teacher to write down details, the benefit of a good decision involving good communication and teacher input ultimately may resolve the problem once and for all.

Schools have assumed a good part of the responsibility for the socialization of children. Behavior or socialization problems often surface in the context of the school or classroom, even though they are caused by outside influences.

Causes of violence, vandalism, and school disruption are numerous: low student self-esteem, insufficient student participation in rule making, divorce, child abuse, neglect, alcoholism, and others.[3]

Antecedent conditions present in schools also influence behavior: authoritarian behavior toward students characterized by oppression and petty rules, teacher disrespect toward students, callousness, disinterest, incompetence, arbitrary and inconsistent rule enforcement, overcrowding, obsolete facilities,

---

[3]Causes and remedies of school conflict and violence are described in "Administrators' Advice: Causes and Remedies of School Conflict and Violence," *NASSP Bulletin*, April 1983, pp.75-79.

low staff morale, drug and alcohol problems among students, gang problems, inadequacy of the curriculum and activity program aggravated by ineffective classroom management skills.

Misbehavior in the school or classroom is often only a symptom of a larger problem troubling the student and thereby causing difficulty for that student, the teacher, and other students. No ideal cure or punishment exists for all types of misbehavior. Special efforts are required, therefore, to pinpoint the actual causes or the motivation for misbehavior before setting out to cure the recalcitrant.

In an era characterized by efforts to solve many of the problems that face society, parents and educators also look for a specialist in schools to cure the ills of a misbehaving student. Today, we use whatever means available to find the cure for a student who cannot, or will not conform to the dictates of the school's code of conduct.

The school is expanding its role, perhaps to compensate for changes in the family and society, and seems to be accepting more and more responsibility for the socialization of children. It is no longer acceptable to refer the unruly student to the parents for reform.

In this transitional period, the school organization can no longer simply legislate appropriate behavior for all students without detailing what will be done to, or with, those who violate stated expectations or standards of behavior. The current emphasis is not exclusively on achieving the mission of the entire school, but rather on focusing on the needs, personality, and problems of the individual student—in particular, the student who requires "special" attention. The school counselor plays a major role in achieving this goal.

The Counselor's Role

The public school counselors wear many hats, some of which denote duties far from those reflected in the specialized training they received. Their commonly described duties are: To plan and evaluate the curriculum; to help students understand and improve themselves; to assist parents in working with their children; and to assist teachers in understanding their students.

The counselor is involved in discipline not as an arm of the discipline office, not as the authority figure of the institution, not even as a partisan advocate of the student. The counselor is a facilitator who helps both student and organization by helping students learn acceptable behavior.

The school counselors are, therefore, called upon to play an increasingly important role in what is termed "developmental counseling." They must guide the students in taking an active part in solving their problems, identifying their influence and control over their behavior and lives, and making conscious decisions to act responsibly. The goal is to establish self-discipline.

The school counselor is in a key position to play the role of student advocate, troubleshooter, motivational specialist, or therapist in minimizing behavior problems in the school organization by providing problem solving for misbehavior patterns. The counselor can help students by teaching them to learn about and adapt to the environment that influences their behavior.

Reality Therapy in a Conference Setting

Glasser's Reality Therapy is an effective method for guiding discipline intervention conferences. Glasser's eight steps, which systematically structure conferences with students, parents, teachers, and administrators during the intervention process, are:

- Make friends with the student
- Ask the student, "What are you doing now?"
- Ask, "Is this behavior helping you?"
- Suggest that the student outline a plan to improve
- Get a commitment
- Accept no excuses
- Do not criticize
- Cooperatively develop a new plan and never give up.

Reality Therapy focuses attention on the students' own real world—on their future. It is a technique that helps to delve into the consciousness of the student in order to clarify behavioral expectations and avoid future mistakes. Criticism is minimized.

While Reality Therapy is by definition therapeutic, it is also a successful intervention technique. The student agrees to identify a blueprint for success and then take the first step in saying he or she will start again. Consequences are identified and must be enforced. Excuses are not accepted and a broken agreement calls for predetermined consequences.

The disciplinarian, using Glasser's techniques, functions as a coach working with the student in a supportive relationship, helping the student avoid painful consequences by establishing a new plan after each failure. The focus is constructive, not negative or critical.

The intervention procedures in effective school discipline programs are probably the most important. Only when disruption and violence are calmly and matter-of-factly stopped at the earliest possible point, can schools experience order and control. Only in a business-like atmosphere where everyone knows what is expected, can anarchy and chaos be avoided.

Intervention is a blood, sweat, and tears experience for everyone involved. It helps students develop self-discipline by guiding their development of conscience until external intervention is no longer required.

Case Study

At Conant High School, a suburban Chicago public secondary school, each suspended student takes part in a counseling period before working with five subject-related tutors on academic assignments. This commitment of time for counselors is based on the counselors' mission to help the student re-enter the school community with an awareness of what he or she did wrong.

The student and counselor discuss an alternative way of behaving to avoid further penalty; the student identifies a specific plan to improve; and the counselor helps the student resolve any problems the student wishes to discuss.

The student, counselor, parents, and administrator in charge of discipline may focus attention on one of several goals to resolve student problems. These goals may include:

1. To prevent or minimize the situation in which a student's personal problems affect and interfere with academic as well as behavioral success
2. To identify for the student how his or her misbehavior is perceived by others
3. To facilitate or re-establish a cooperative relationship between teachers and student, parent and student, etc.
4. To teach the student the meaning of self-motivation toward self-discipline and the benefits of acting in this manner
5. To assist the student in understanding him or herself, goals, feelings, aspirations, and the relationship of school and learning to those factors
6. To identify alternative behaviors which are acceptable to teachers, administrators, and peers
7. To help the student develop a plan to improve his or her behavior in a systematic manner and identify the consequences of failing to live up to that plan
8. To help the student understand the organizational and institutional reasoning behind the school's policies, procedures, and rules
9. To provide a helpful and non-threatening adult to listen to a student's concerns and suggestions to change or improve the school rules or organization.

Summary

Discipline efforts in schools need not be viewed as punitive or destructive. In fact, when the school personnel take the position that students are not simply miniature adults but are developing members of a society who need guidance and help, school discipline becomes a "constructive" effort.

Discipline in schools is everyone's business. Everyone is affected by disruptive, violent, and misbehaving students. When a student is unable or unwilling to behave in an acceptable manner, the school also, in a sense, fails. Student misbehavior is an opportunity for counselors, students, parents, teachers, and administrators to work together for the good of each student and the entire school organization.

The role of the school counselor should be clarified. Even

though some would say it is not fair to spend so much time and effort on the unruly students, their particular problems will not go away without special efforts. Counselors can have a positive rapport with all students when they help identify and resolve the causes of student misbehavior.

Concerned administrators and teachers can help students grow intellectually and socially by providing a no-nonsense, loving, and supportive atmosphere built upon application of intervention techniques whenever the need arises.[4]

Intervention helps students develop self-discipline by guiding their development of conscience until the point occurs when external intervention is no longer required.

[4]Arthur C. Johnson in the May 1979 *NASSP Bulletin* amplified this position in "Toughness: The Answer to Discipline Problems," pp. 130-131.

Chapter 8

Launching a Schoolwide Climate Improvement Project: Focusing on Effective Discipline

To counter symptoms of a discipline problem at Conant High School near Chicago, a committee was organized to address the following concerns:

1. Several teachers said they were not being supported by the administration in providing a positive school tone/ climate.
2. Some faculty members were frustrated that existing discipline rules and policies were not uniformly applied by all teachers. Some teachers allegedly ignored student violations of school rules.
3. Some students did not seem to know what classroom behavior or school behavior was expected of them.

One volunteer representative from each of the school's academic departments, a counselor, and three assistant principals served on the discipline committee, which met before school. The assistant principal in charge of the discipline office was the committee chairperson.

First Meeting

The first meeting's agenda provided for a general airing of faculty members' perspectives about discipline problems in the school. The issues were listed and committee members were then asked to poll their departments in ranking the top five discipline problem areas in each of two categories: class-related problems and out-of-class problems.

Second Meeting

The highest-ranking problems fit into four general categories: integrity, conduct, responsibility, and respect.

Four subcommittees were formed to explore answers to the following questions:

1. How will the school teach desired behavior to students?
2. What steps should the teacher take when he or she observes unacceptable behavior?
3. What steps will the administrator take when the student is referred to the discipline office?

After the first two discipline committee meetings, some tentative conclusions were reached:

1. Inappropriate student behavior affects good school tone and makes it difficult for students to learn and teachers to teach.
2. It is unreasonable to expect acceptable behavior if students do not know what acceptable behavior is.
3. Communication of expected behavior to students, staff, and parents is the foundation of good discipline.
4. To improve student behavior, we must communicate expected behavior to students.
5. We must communicate expected behavior to parents early in the year and enlist their support and cooperation.
6. We must communicate our expectations to the staff regarding standards for student behavior.
7. To be effective, we must expect that every staff member will enforce these student expectations consistently. We recognize that we all have the responsibility to teach appropriate behavior by example.

8. Administrative staff must support teacher staff by letting teachers know what steps to take to correct inappropriate behavior and by letting staff know how they will be backed up in the discipline office.
9. Administrative staff must be firm and consistent in their enforcement of expected behavior.
10. Communication of appropriate school behavior and the socialization of students must be an ongoing process that occurs throughout the school year.

Committee Recommendations

Within a month, the following comprehensive plan for improving the school and classroom discipline program was adopted:

1. Distribute information to faculty members to orient them to suggested steps for enforcing appropriate behavior in the classroom and hallways, and to explain what kind of follow-up could be expected from administrators when a student is referred to the office.
2. Develop opportunities to communicate expectations and standards of student behavior to the entire staff through faculty meetings and a slide/tape program.
3. Develop opportunities to orient all students regarding behavioral expectations and consequences of misbehavior, including the following components:
   - Student handbook containing complete descriptions of rules and regulations
   - A sound/slide tape presentation on student rights and responsibilities
   - A sound/slide tape presentation on the value of school discipline and a review of behavioral expectations in a two-day presentation.
   - Teacher explanations of expected behavior during the first day of each semester using a prepared script for every class period.
4. Development of a plan to inform parents concerning behavioral standards of school discipline through:
   - Newsletters from principals
   - Open house presentation

- Freshman orientation night for parents
- Student handbook.
5. Development of a systematic procedure for teachers to use in dealing with minor but annoying disruptive discipline problems in the classroom. This sequential ladder utilized various levels of punishment or consequences.

Guidelines for Staff on Systematic Discipline Enforcement

The staff guidelines for systematic discipline enforcement were given to teachers:

I. *Conduct*
   Staff responsibility:
   - Set an example in word, deed, appearance
   - Model the behavior expected of students
   - Know and enforce the rules

Student Responsibility Behavior Expectation	Teacher Remediation Responsibility	Administrator Remediation Responsibility
· Smoke only in smoking area	Refer to office	Health seminar or suspension
· No running in hall	Warn, tell to walk	Warn, 1 detention
· No excessive show of affection	Warn, tell to part	Warn, parent contact
· Appropriate dress	Suggest attire	Warn, parent contact
· No obscene gestures or profanity	Refer to office	Suspension
· No possession/use of alcohol or drugs	Bring to office	5-day suspension
· No selling drugs	Bring to office	Expulsion hearing
· Show I.D. when asked	Refer to office	Suspension

II. *Integrity*
   Staff Responsibility:
   - Set an example to your students
   - Say what you mean and mean what you say
   - Model the behavior

· Be honest in dealing with staff	Call parent; if behavior continues, refer to office	Up to 10-day suspension

• Do not cheat on homework, tests, projects	Refer to office, give a zero on work	Referral; after second incident student is dropped from class
• Do not steal	Refer to office	Suspension up to 10 days; victim may file police complaint
• Do not forge school documents	Refer to office	Suspension

III. *Responsibility*
Staff responsibility:
- Model the behavior
- Set an example—be on time to class; show you're prepared to teach; make each day important for the student to be there

• Be in class daily	Have student make up work	After 8 absences, a course reduction
• Be on time	Send to office if not seated when bell rings	Detentions on 4th and 5th tardy; 6th tardy—parent phone conference; 7th tardy—possible suspension preceding parent conference; class dropped after 7th
• Be prepared to work when the bell rings	After-class conference, follow management form	Suspension from class, parent conference
• Bring materials to class each day	After-class conference, follow management form	Suspension from class, parent conference

IV. *Respect*
Staff responsibility:
- Set an example by respecting your profession
- Show pride in your work and school
- Teach proper behavior at school activities

• Respect one's self and others	Conference with student; call parent if acts continue	Parent contact, and/or class suspension
• Respect the school's property and others'	Refer to office for vandalism	Suspension and restitution
• Respect the school's traditions while attending activities	Refer to office for misbehavior suspension	Social probation then school

Results and Commentary

The results of the discipline renewal program were dramatic. The discipline office reported 2,670 fewer referrals during the first year of the new program. This represents approximately a 40 percent decrease.

The discipline office enjoyed a good reputation, perhaps due to the following:

- Efficiency. Something was done soon and was followed up.
- Organization. Teachers knew and used discipline office procedures to refer a student to an administrator.
- Coordination. Three students seeing three different administrators could expect the same penalty.
- Communication. It was personal. A written notice was sent to teachers and parents within 24 hours of referral following a decision.
- Consistency. Teachers were told what to expect from the administrator as a result of the discipline committee recommendations.
- Consideration. Most teachers used the office for serious discipline problems only. Seldom did teachers refer students for talking or being unprepared. Guidelines for determining how and when to refer students to the office were included in the policy handbook.

A classroom management form that requested teacher or parent contact prior to referral to the administrator was also developed. The administrator in the discipline office could, therefore, address the more extreme cases and spend more time with the chronic problem students.

Summary

The discipline committee accomplished several important tasks:

1. Projected an attitude that *together* they could accomplish a common goal: a well-disciplined school.
2. Clarified the responsibilities of the participants in the school's discipline program.
3. Worked together in identifying what discipline policies would/should be appropriate.

APPENDICES

APPENDIX A
CLASSROOM BEHAVIOR MANAGEMENT FORM

Student Name _____ Serial No. _____ Year _____

Teacher _____ Subject _____ Period _____

The above student's behavior has been disturbing the class and my ability to teach. Specifically, the problem is:

_____

_____

_____

As the classroom teacher, I have taken the following steps to correct the problem.

Step 1: An *AFTER-CLASS DISCUSSION* was held on _____ with the student regarding the above problem. The student reaction to the problem and my suggestions for improvement were:
____ Favorable   ____ Unfavorable   ____ No reaction

_____   _____
Teacher Signature   Student Signature

Step 2: A *FORMAL TEACHER/STUDENT CONFERENCE* was held on _____ at _____. The problem was again discussed and the _(Date)_ _(Time)_ student warned that further misbehavior would result in a referral to office 105. The student reaction to my suggestions for improvement were:
____ Favorable   ____ Unfavorable   ____ No reaction

_____   _____
Teacher Signature   Student Signature

Step 3: *PARENT PHONE CONTACT* was made on _ Phone Number _ The parent was advised of the problems and the steps taken thus far by the teacher to remedy the problem. The parent's support was requested. Parent reaction was:
_____ Positive   _____ Neutral   _____ No reaction

Step 4: The following *RESOURCE PEOPLE* were consulted:
A. Department Chairman: He/she made the following recommendations:

B. Guidance Counselor: He/she provided the following assistance:

_____

Step 5: THE PROBLEM PERSISTS. I want this student to be seen by an *ASSISTANT PRINCIPAL*. Send this form and the student to 105.

_____

_____

| _____ | _____ |
| Date, Time Student Sent | Teacher Signature |

To   The Assistant Principal will write a referral, copies of
Teacher: which will be sent to you and the parent. You are urged
         to contact the Discipline Office at the end of the day to
         learn of the disposition of this matter.

APPENDIX B
BEHAVIOR MANAGEMENT ACTION PLAN

I. Restate the problem in specific terms:
    (teacher viewpoint)

II. Restate the problem in specific terms:
    (student viewpoint)

III. Action Plan/Behavior agreement:
    (A commitment to improve)
    Provide a description of what the student should do differently

IV. Consequences:
    State the consequences of not abiding by the agreement in III above.

APPENDIX C
BEHAVIOR CONTRACT

Class _____

Teacher _____

Date _____

I, _____ understand that if I wish to remain in class and have the opportunity to receive credit, I must abide by the following rules:

1. I must be in my seat and quiet when the bell rings.

2. I must be in class every day with my textbook, notebook, and pen or sharpened pencil.

3. I must not disturb others by talking or disruptive behavior during class announcements, lectures, discussions, or films. I will not call out answers or make comments without permission.

4. I will make no obscene comments during class.

5. I must remain in my seat during class, except during labs. I will remain in my seat until dismissed by the teacher at the end of the period.

6. Other _____

If I do not abide by the above rules, I understand I will face suspension and/or drop of the class.

_____
(Student's Signature)

_____
(Witness-Assistant Principal)

cc: Parent
    Teacher
    Student
    Discipline file

APPENDIX D
IN-SCHOOL SUSPENSION

Purpose

The primary purpose of the In-School Suspension Center (I.S.S.) is to offer a structured, supervised program to suspended students and their parents in lieu of an unsupervised, unstructured out-of-school suspension. The student who is assigned to the suspension center will be in an educational environment with total isolation from his peers. It is felt that the in-school suspension program will have a positive effect on students' general school attitude and behavior and help students who are far behind on their academic studies. Since students dislike this approach, the program serves as a "deterrent" for students who avoid misbehavior in light of a particularly offensive penalty.

Eligibility

The opportunity for a student to participate in the I.S.S. program will be at the discretion of the administrator in charge of the student's discipline. The administrator will evaluate each case individually as to whether the alternative to "out-of-school suspension" will be offered. The nature, number, and seriousness of the offenses will be the determining factors coupled with a concern and judgment whether the student can profit from the I.S.S. program. In addition, the administrator may seek the opinions of the counselor, special service personnel familiar with the student, as well as teacher recommendations, before an eligibility decision is made.

Major Program Characteristics

1. The student earns his way back into the regular school environment by meeting specific requirements.
2. Re-entry into the regular school program is based on the student's performance in fulfilling the student's responsibilities to the program.

3. A specific room will be available for a maximum of five to six students where learning can take place in a controlled setting.
4. Teachers will provide education that is coordinated with the student's classes.

Basic Principles

1. A specific room is provided for I.S.S. participants. A characteristic of the I.S.S. program is the restriction of the student's social life within the school. The restriction of social activities is complete:

    a. Movement to and from the I.S.S. program is at designated times.
    b. If lunch is desired, the I.S.S. participant will bring his own lunch.
    c. Washroom privileges will be given only at times other than regular passing times and under the direct supervision of a teacher.
    d. During the student's time in the I.S.S., the student will not be able to talk, sleep, or walk around.
    e. The student is restricted from all assemblies and after-school activities until re-entry is earned.

2. Specific instructions are given for all assignments with the goal of helping the student become better adjusted to tasks required of him in the regular school setting. The completion of all class work in a manner satisfactory to the supervisory personnel is absolutely necessary for the student to gain re-entry into regular school programs.

3. Re-entry is based on personal performance in the I.S.S. An important objective of the program is to help participants to look at themselves and the reasons for their presence in the program. Through positive professional contact with teachers and counselor, it is anticipated that some "inner reflection" can be a positive stepping stone to getting the student back on track. Goal setting will be incorporated in the re-entry process along with the student's general attitude and cooperation while participating.

4. In-school suspension center supervisors are teachers who share the goal of helping the students with "behavior prob-

lems." Some of the objectives of personnel in the suspension center are as follows:

a. To help develop a trust relationship with the student by demonstrating understanding and acceptance within social and educational limitations.
b. To bring out student frustrations and help overcome them.
c. To emphasize the value of completing a task in an allotted time limit in a neat and correct manner.

It is critical that supervisors of the I.S.S. be totally dedicated to the philosophy of the in-school suspension center. The supervisors will be carefully screened before they are assigned to the center.

APPENDIX E
MONTHLY DISCIPLINE REPORT

SCHOOL _____ DATE _____

REFERRALS	NO. OF REFERRALS		SUSPENSIONS			
	This Month	Year-to-date	Month Number	Days	Year-to-date Number	Days
Academic—Habitual Lack of Work, Poor Attitude						
Alcohol Abuse						
Cheating/Lying/Forgery						
Dangerous Behavior— Misconduct (Horseplay in Halls, Bus)						
Detention Violation— (No show, etc.)						
Disturbance—(Class/ Hall/Bus/Campus)						

Drug Abuse	
Fighting	
Insubordination	
Option & Off-Campus Violation	
Profanity/Obscenity	
Smoking	
Tardiness-5th or more	
Theft	
Truancy-Class/Study Hall	
Truancy-School (all day)	
Unauthorized Absence-1st Class	
Vandalism	
Other (Explain)	

TOTAL

Truancy Referrals to County/Court

	NO. OF REFERRALS		SUSPENSIONS		
	Month	Year-to-date	Number	Days	Number	Days
Freshmen						
Sophomores						
Juniors						
Seniors						

TOTAL

Monthly number _____ of students suspended zero (0) days because of successful parent conferences.

The last column entitled SUSPENSIONS reflects the *NUMBER* of incidents and the *NUMBER* of days resulting from that category of suspensions. FOR EXAMPLE: For *Alcohol Abuse* you may have 3 students (number) suspended for a total (13) days under month.

This report is to arrive in the Assistant Superintendent's Office no later than one week after the first of each month.

APPENDIX F

TOWNSHIP HIGH SCHOOL DISTRICT 211

Administrative Center

DISCIPLINE PHILOSOPHY, GOALS, AND OBJECTIVES

High School District 211 discipline policies and procedures are the product of common understandings and society's expectations of our schools. If our democratic society is to flourish, and our ways of living and believing to endure, we need young people who cherish, understand, and practice these ideals above personal gratification.

School discipline should protect and nurture the physical, social, mental, and emotional growth of its youth. Regulations are made, first, to protect persons and property, and second, to protect the right to participate in every facet of the educational program. The schools' discipline policies reflect an understanding of adolescent human maturation. The schools' policies specifically limit the opportunity of any individual to interrupt another student's educational growth. School policies also protect the student who might choose to interfere with his own educational growth. As each student proceeds through his high school years, greater levels of self-control are expected. We believe discipline exists to make possible a good educational program and to protect the welfare of those who participate in the program. To this end we recognize four axioms:

1. Discipline policies and procedures recognize the inherent dignity and rights of each individual.
2. Discipline policies and procedures focus upon devotion to humanitarian principles and ideals and loyalty to the principles of freedom, justice, and equality.

3. Discipline policies and procedures serve to direct behavior and yet encourage personal effort extended toward self-direction.

4. Discipline policies and procedures strive for student recognition and understanding in that one often has to subjugate one's personal inclinations, whims, comforts, and even some liberties to achieve greater goals than personal ones.

Those charged with the responsibility for guiding students who misbehave recognize and accept society's challenge and trust. Each disciplinarian is an example of the democratic process in action. Individual students must be regarded as having young minds not yet adult. Actions must be taken in accordance with each individual's best interest while considering the welfare of the school's society. Disciplinarians should, therefore, subscribe to the following democratic principles and goals to guide their practices as they help young people grow toward self-direction and self-fulfillment.

1. All students have worth and dignity.
   a. strive to use positive ways of guidance which help communicate belief in self-worth.
   b. recognize student needs in relation to their personal histories.
2. All students have the capacity to learn cooperation and respect for others.
   a. provide a climate in which mutual respect and trust are possible.
   b. provide opportunities for understanding by encouraging communication between people.

3. All students should understand the policies which affect them.
   a. provide a variety of opportunities to students for familiarization with policies and procedures.
   b. provide students the reasons for policies and procedures.
   c. provide opportunities for students' growth in democratic government by providing channels for their concerns and suggestions.

    d. provide an opportunity for students to foresee the consequences of their behavior.

4. All students with special needs should be referred to those specifically trained to help them.

    a. approach student behaviors individually, searching for causes while attempting to change unacceptable behavior.

    b. assist young people in understanding the reasons for their own behavior and develop more effective ways of resolving conflicts.

    c. recognize, in some instances, greater professional expertise and facilities exist outside the school.

5. Parents must accept a participating role with that of the school and its staff in preparing children for productive and fulfilling lives.

    a. provide direction to staff and involve parents in adjusting student misbehavior.

    b. provide opportunities for parents and students to jointly solve problems.

6. Some parents and students can create problems which are damaging to themselves or to the school's society.

    a. make recommendations and take action which preserves the school's society.

    b. make recommendations and take action which reduces self-damaging actions.

APPENDIX G

HOFFMAN ESTATES HIGH SCHOOL
MODERN LANGUAGE DEPARTMENT

CLASSROOM STANDARDS

I. BE PRESENT AND ON TIME

    A. Good attendance is important to succeed in a language class. Explanation/participation in listening, reading, speaking, and writing are daily components in a language classroom.

    B. A truancy will result in an F for the work for that day.

    C. An unauthorized absence will result in a grade reduction of the work for the day.

    D. A pre-excused/school-related absence means the student should have work for the day completed before being excused. Teacher discretion may allow variation. The student should, however, be prepared to take a quiz or test should it fall on the day of his/her return.

    E. If a student is absent for several days, he/she should follow the assignment sheet. If there are questions regarding the work assigned, the student should call his/her teacher for clarification.

    F. The tardy policy will be enforced by the classroom teacher (room/seat at teacher discretion). The student is to remain in his/her seat until the dismissal bell rings.

II. BRING LEARNING MATERIALS

    A. The student is expected to come to class with pen-/pencil, paper, text, notebook/folder, lab book (if applicable).

B. Passes to lockers for the above materials will not be issued.

III. RESPECT OTHER PEOPLE AND THEIR PROPERTY

A. At all times the student should act with courtesy toward teachers and other students. Both their actions and words should reflect this courtesy.
B. The student is responsible to keep all school property (books, classroom materials) in good condition.
C. The student will exhibit proper classroom behavior which includes:
   1. No eating in class.
   2. No feet on desks, book racks.
   3. No writing on desks or bulletin boards.
   4. No tossing paper on the floor.
   5. No work other than the work for this class being done during the class.
   6. No cheating.

IV. BE PREPARED TO PARTICIPATE

A. Grading
   1. Determination of the quarter
      a. Quizzes (1/3)
      b. Exams (1/3)
      c. Oral (oral quizzes, participation, effort, attitude, homework) (1/3). /Daily attendance is important to achieve maximum performance. Attitude and effort maximize performance as well.
   2. Variations of the above fractions may occur in upper level courses. Special projects, book reports, etc., may be included and assigned a value.
B. Homework
   1. The student is expected to come to class with learning materials listed under Part II. Assignment sheets will be prepared regularly by the teacher so that the student will always be informed of his/her daily responsibility.

2. If a student accumulates 3 no-homeworks during the course of a 9-week period, the teacher may request an after-school or class conference with the student to discuss the student's problem. A call or report to parents may result for subsequent no-homeworks.
3. The student's homework grade for the 9-week period will be lowered for the number of no-homeworks beyond 3.

C. Tutoring/conferences after school
1. The teacher or student should request a conference at least 24 hours in advance.
2. The student should be present at the conference or arrange for another meeting if there is a conflict with previous plans.
3. If the student does not arrive for the scheduled conference he/she will be sent from class (at the beginning of the hour on the following day) to the appropriate assistant principal for disciplinary action due to insubordination.

APPENDIX H

STUDENT ORIENTATION SCHEDULE

Office of the Assistant Principal

TO: ALL TEACHERS
FR:
RE: REMINDER ORIENTATION FOR STUDENT BEHAVIOR

NOTE TO TEACHERS

We are requesting that each teacher play an important role in reaffirming essential points regarding student behavior. As each teacher claims responsibility to enforce accepted rules, we CAN create a *consistent* environment where students know how to behave and what to expect as consequences for misbehaving.

The following orientation schedule has been developed and should be discussed by *each teacher* on Tuesday, January 29, 1985. Approximately 10 minutes should be taken by the teacher each period to cover the listed topics. A script is provided.

During periods 4, 5, 6 a review of all policy (as per attached pages) ensures that the majority of students will have been given our expectations. Each teacher is encouraged to clarify his/her *own classroom* expectations also including:

1. You will treat each student with respect and you expect to be treated the same in return.
2. Students have a responsibility to:
   a. Keep regular attendance
   b. Be on time to class
   c. Be honest in their dealings with other students and with you (i.e. students should do and turn in their own work. Cheating will not be tolerated.)
   d. Come prepared to class and participate in class.

STUDENT ORIENTATION SCHEDULE

Period 1
Why Rules?
Smoking Policy
Student I.D.
Bus Behavior

Period 2
Unacceptable Class or Hall Behavior
Fighting
Student Dressing/Grooming
Fire Drill Behavior

Period 3
Attendance
Tardy Policy
Prearranged Absences
After School Teacher Conference
Library Overdues

Period 4,5,6
Cafeteria Behavior
Off-Campus Lunch Policy and Leaving Campus
Attendance
Tardy Policy
Prearranged Absences
Smoking Policy

Period 7
Behavior at School Events
Cougar Code of Conduct
Lockers
Radios

Period 8
Nurse
Courtesy and Respect
Questions/Highlight
Attendance and Tardy Procedure

APPENDIX I
SCRIPT FOR STUDENT ORIENTATION

PERIOD 1

A. Why Rules?

Rules and procedures are a part of life no matter where we work or attend school. Knowing what is expected of us makes our day a lot easier. When rules are followed, the school is a more orderly place in which we can learn and work.

To help you understand the school's expectations of you regarding behavior and attendance, a STUDENT-PARENT CALENDAR/HANDBOOK was mailed to you. That handbook explains the school's expectations in great detail. We hope you and your parents have read it carefully.

Our reason for reviewing these guidelines is to help make sure you don't find yourself giving an excuse "I didn't know." *IGNORANCE OF RULES cannot be used as an excuse.*

B. Smoking Policy

Students may smoke only in the *designated* smoking area during the hours of 7:30-3:30. You must have parent permission and a properly coded school I.D. to be in this area. The smoking area is located outside the band hallway. Smoking is *prohibited* in the parking lot, outside school entrances, in washrooms, or anyplace on school property. This includes before and after school hours. It includes NO SMOKING in private cars while on campus or NO SMOKING on the school bus.

C. Student I.D. (Identification Cards)

Carry your I.D. card with you at all times. You must show and/or surrender your I.D. card to *any staff member* requesting it—whether it be a teacher, student supervisor, or custodian. Failure to have an I.D. or to show it when asked will result in disciplinary action such as loss of option privileges, parent contact, or detention.

You need an I.D. to:

1. Enter the school bus.
2. Check out library materials.
3. Attend school activities and athletic events.
4. Make up tests in the Test Make-Up Room (Room 106).
5. Enter the smoking area.
6. Leave campus with off-campus privilege.
7. Receive a tardy.
8. Leave study hall to go on option if you are a junior or senior.

(SHOULD YOU LOSE YOUR I.D., YOU MUST RE-PLACE IT.)

Replacement I.D. procedure is: The student reports to the Audio Visual Room on Tuesdays and Thursdays, 7:30-9:00. The cost of replacement is $1.00 and $2.00 on the second replacement.

PERIOD 2

A. *Staying After School:*

A teacher may request you to stay after school to discuss a behavior problem or have you do academic work. As long as the student has been given a *24 hour* notice by the teacher, the student *must* attend the after-school conference. Failure to attend will result in a referral to the assistant principal who will take disciplinary action.